St. Joseph,
Pray for Us

St. Joseph, Pray for Us

Meditations and Prayers

*On the 150th Anniversary
of the Proclamation
of St. Joseph as Patron of the
Universal Church*

Pope Francis

LIBRERIA
EDITRICE
VATICANA

PAULIST PRESS

Library of Congress Control Number: 2021932099

ISBN: 978-0-8091-5582-8 (paperback)
ISBN: 978-1-58768-986-4 (e-book)

Published by Paulist Press
997 Macarthur Boulevard
Mahwah, New Jersey 07430
www.paulistpress.com

In collaboration with Libreria Editrice Vaticana
00120 Città del Vaticano
Tel. 06.698.45780
Email: commerciale.lev@spc.va
www.vatican.va
www.libreriaeditricevaticana.va

Printed and bound in the United States of America

Contents

"If anyone cannot find a master to teach him how to pray, let him take this glorious saint as his master and he will not go astray."
—St. Teresa of Avila

Preface

POPE FRANCIS wrote a letter about St. Joseph titled *Patris Corde*. In his own words, "The aim of this Apostolic Letter is to increase our love for this great saint, to encourage us to implore his intercession and to imitate his virtues and his zeal."

The purpose of this book is to provide the opportunity to prayerfully reflect on excerpts[1] from these words from Pope Francis and see how to apply them in our own lives.

Finally, we join the Holy Father in praying to this great saint, for our needs, the needs of the whole Church, and the needs of all the world.

---

1. The full text of *Patris Corde* is available on the Vatican website: www.vatican.va.

The Story of St. Joseph

With a father's heart:
that is how Joseph loved Jesus,
whom all four Gospels refer to as
"the son of Joseph."

MATTHEW AND LUKE, the two Evangelists who speak most of Joseph, tell us very little, yet enough for us to appreciate what sort of father he was, and the mission entrusted to him by God's providence.

We know that Joseph was a lowly carpenter (cf. Mt 13:55), betrothed to Mary (cf. Mt 1:18; Lk 1:27). He was a "just man" (Mt 1:19), ever ready to carry out God's will as revealed to him in the Law (cf. Lk 2:22.27.39) and through four dreams (cf. Mt 1:20; 2:13.19.22). After a long and tiring journey from Nazareth to Bethlehem, he beheld the birth of the Messiah in a stable, since "there was no place for them" elsewhere (cf. Lk 2:7). He witnessed the adoration of the shepherds (cf. Lk 2:8–20) and the Magi (cf. Mt 2:1–12), who represented respectively the people of Israel and the pagan peoples.

Joseph had the courage to become the legal father of Jesus, to whom he gave the name revealed by the angel: "You shall call his name Jesus, for he will save his people from their sins" (Mt 1:21). As we know, for ancient peoples, to give a name to a person or to a thing, as Adam did in the account in the Book of Genesis (cf. 2:19–20), was to establish a relationship.

In the Temple, forty days after Jesus' birth, Joseph and Mary offered their child to the Lord and listened with amazement to Simeon's prophecy concerning Jesus and his Mother (cf. Lk 2:22–35). To protect Jesus from Herod, Joseph dwelt as a foreigner in Egypt (cf. Mt 2:13–18). After returning to his own country, he led a hidden life in the tiny and obscure village of Nazareth in Galilee, far from Bethlehem, his ancestral town, and from Jerusalem and the Temple. Of Nazareth it was said, "No prophet is to rise" (cf. Jn 7:52) and indeed, "Can anything good come out of Nazareth?" (cf. Jn 1:46). When, during a pilgrimage to Jerusalem, Joseph and Mary lost track of the twelve-year-old Jesus, they anxiously sought him out and they found him in the Temple, in discussion with the doctors of the Law (cf. Lk 2:41–50).

After Mary, the Mother of God, no saint is mentioned more frequently in the papal magisterium than Joseph, her spouse. My Predecessors reflected on the message contained in the limited information handed down by the Gospels in order to appreciate more fully his central role in the history of salvation. Blessed *Pius IX* declared him "Patron of the Catholic Church," Venerable *Pius XII* proposed him as "Patron of Workers" and *Saint John Paul II* as "Guardian of the Redeemer." Saint Joseph is universally invoked as the "patron of a happy death."

Meditations

I WOULD LIKE to share some personal reflections on this extraordinary figure, so close to our own human experience. For, as Jesus says, "out of the abundance of the heart the mouth speaks" (Mt 12:34).

My desire to do so increased during these months of pandemic, when we experienced, amid the crisis, how "our lives are woven together and sustained by ordinary people, people often overlooked. People who do not appear in newspaper and magazine headlines, or on the latest television show, yet in these very days are surely shaping the decisive events of our history. Doctors, nurses, storekeepers and supermarket workers, cleaning personnel, caregivers, transport workers, men and women working to provide essential services and public safety, volunteers, priests, men and women religious, and so very many others. They understood that no one is saved alone...

How many people daily exercise patience and offer hope, taking care to spread not panic, but shared responsibility. How many fathers, mothers, grandparents and teachers are showing our children, in small everyday ways, how to accept and deal with a crisis by adjusting their routines, looking ahead and encouraging the practice of prayer. How many are praying, making sacrifices and interceding for the good of all."

Each of us can discover in Joseph—the man who goes unnoticed, a daily, discreet and hidden presence—an intercessor, a support and a guide in times of trouble. Saint Joseph reminds us that those who appear hidden or in the shadows can play an incomparable role in the history of salvation. A word of recognition and of gratitude is due to them all.

JOSEPH SAW JESUS grow daily "in wisdom and in years and in divine and human favor" (Lk 2:52). As the Lord had done with Israel, so Joseph did with Jesus: he taught him to walk, taking him by the hand; he was for him like a father who raises an infant to his cheeks, bending down to him and feeding him (cf. Hos 11:3–4).

In Joseph, Jesus saw the tender love of God: "As a father has compassion for his children, so the Lord has compassion for those who fear him" (Ps 103:13).

THE EVIL ONE makes us see and condemn our frailty, whereas the Spirit brings it to light with tender love. Tenderness is the best way to touch the frailty within us. Pointing fingers and judging others are frequently signs of an inability to accept our own weaknesses, our own frailty. Only tender love will save us from the snares of the accuser (cf. Rev 12:10). That is why it is so important to encounter God's mercy, especially in the Sacrament of Reconciliation, where we experience his truth and tenderness.

PARADOXICALLY, the evil one can also speak the truth to us, yet he does so only to condemn us. We know that God's truth does not condemn, but instead welcomes, embraces, sustains and forgives us. That truth always presents itself to us like the merciful father in Jesus' parable (cf. Lk 15:11–32). It comes out to meet us, restores our dignity, sets us back on our feet and rejoices for us, for, as the father says: "This my son was dead and is alive again; he was lost and is found" (v. 24).

EVEN THROUGH Joseph's fears, God's will, his history and his plan were at work. Joseph, then, teaches us that faith in God includes believing that he can work even through our fears, our frailties and our weaknesses. He also teaches us that amid the tempests of life, we must never be afraid to let the Lord steer our course. At times, we want to be in complete control, yet God always sees the bigger picture.

AS HE HAD DONE with Mary, God revealed his saving plan to Joseph. He did so by using dreams, which in the Bible and among all ancient peoples, were considered a way for him to make his will known.

Joseph was deeply troubled by Mary's mysterious pregnancy. He did not want to "expose her to public disgrace," *[14]* so he decided to "dismiss her quietly" (Mt 1:19).

In the first dream, an angel helps him resolve his grave dilemma: "Do not be afraid to take Mary as your wife, for the child conceived in her is from the Holy Spirit. She will bear a son, and you are to name him Jesus, for he will save his people from their sins" (Mt 1:20–21). Joseph's response was immediate: "When Joseph awoke from sleep, he did as the angel of the Lord commanded him" (Mt 1:24). Obedience made it possible for him to surmount his difficulties and spare Mary.

IN THE SECOND dream, the angel tells Joseph: "Get up, take the child and his mother, and flee to Egypt, and remain there until I tell you; for Herod is about to search for the child, to destroy him" (Mt 2:13). Joseph did not hesitate to obey, regardless of the hardship involved: "He got up, took the child and his mother by night, and went to Egypt, and remained there until the death of Herod" (Mt 2:14–15).

IN EGYPT, Joseph awaited with patient trust the angel's notice that he could safely return home. In a third dream, the angel told him that those who sought to kill the child were dead and ordered him to rise, take the child and his mother, and return to the land of Israel (cf. Mt 2:19–20). Once again, Joseph promptly obeyed. "He got up, took the child and his mother, and went to the land of Israel" (Mt 2:21).

During the return journey, "when Joseph heard that Archelaus was ruling over Judea in place of his father Herod, he was afraid to go there. After being warned in a dream"—now for the fourth time—"he went away to the district of Galilee. There he made his home in a town called Nazareth" (Mt 2:22–23).

All this makes it clear that "Saint Joseph was called by God to serve the person and mission of Jesus directly through the exercise of his fatherhood" and that in this way, "he cooperated in the fullness of time in the great mystery of salvation and is truly a minister of salvation."

JOSEPH ACCEPTED Mary unconditionally. He trusted in the angel's words. "The nobility of Joseph's heart is such that what he learned from the law he made dependent on charity. Today, in our world where psychological, verbal and physical violence towards women is so evident, Joseph appears as the figure of a respectful and sensitive man. Even though he does not understand the bigger picture, he makes a decision to protect Mary's good name, her dignity and her life. In his hesitation about how best to act, God helped him by enlightening his judgment."

OFTEN IN LIFE, things happen whose meaning we do not understand. Our first reaction is frequently one of disappointment and rebellion. Joseph set aside his own ideas in order to accept the course of events and, mysterious as they seemed, to embrace them, take responsibility for them and make them part of his own history. Unless we are reconciled with our own history, we will be unable to take a single step forward, for we will always remain hostage to our expectations and the disappointments that follow.

THE SPIRITUAL PATH that Joseph traces for us is not one that explains but accepts. Only as a result of this acceptance, this reconciliation, can we begin to glimpse a broader history, a deeper meaning. We can almost hear an echo of the impassioned reply of Job to his wife, who had urged him to rebel against the evil he endured: "Shall we receive the good at the hand of God, and not receive the bad?" (Job 2:10).

Joseph is certainly not passively resigned, but courageously and firmly proactive. In our own lives, acceptance and welcome can be an expression of the Holy Spirit's gift of fortitude. Only the Lord can give us the strength needed to accept life as it is, with all its contradictions, frustrations and disappointments.

Jesus' appearance in our midst is a gift from the Father, which makes it possible for each of us to be reconciled to the flesh of our own history, even when we fail to understand it completely.

JUST AS GOD told Joseph: "Son of David, do not be afraid!" (Mt 1:20), so he seems to tell us: "Do not be afraid!" We need to set aside all anger and disappointment, and to embrace the way things are, even when they do not turn out as we wish. Not with mere resignation but with hope and courage. In this way, we become open to a deeper meaning. Our lives can be miraculously reborn if we find the courage to live them in accordance with the Gospel. It does not matter if everything seems to have gone wrong or some things can no longer be fixed. God can make flowers spring up from stony ground. Even if our heart condemns us, "God is greater than our hearts, and he knows everything" (1 Jn 3:20).

HERE, ONCE AGAIN, we encounter that Christian realism which rejects nothing that exists. Reality, in its mysterious and irreducible complexity, is the bearer of existential meaning, with all its lights and shadows. Thus, the Apostle Paul can say: "We know that all things work together for good, for those who love God" (Rom 8:28). To which Saint Augustine adds, "even that which is called evil (*etiam illud quod malum dicitur*)." In this greater perspective, faith gives meaning to every event, however happy or sad.

Nor should we ever think that believing means finding facile and comforting solutions. The faith Christ taught us is what we see in Saint Joseph. He did not look for shortcuts, but confronted reality with open eyes and accepted personal responsibility for it.

JOSEPH'S ATTITUDE encourages us to accept and welcome others as they are, without exception, and to show special concern for the weak, for God chooses what is weak (cf. 1 Cor 1:27). He is the "Father of orphans and protector of widows" (Ps 68:6), who commands us to love the stranger in our midst. I like to think that it was from Saint Joseph that Jesus drew inspiration for the parable of the prodigal son and the merciful father (cf. Lk 15:11–32).

IF THE FIRST stage of all true interior healing is to accept our personal history and embrace even the things in life that we did not choose, we must now add another important element: creative courage. This emerges especially in the way we deal with difficulties. In the face of difficulty, we can either give up and walk away, or somehow engage with it. At times, difficulties bring out resources we did not even think we had.

GOD ACTS THROUGH events and people. Joseph was the man chosen by God to guide the beginnings of the history of redemption. He was the true "miracle" by which God saves the child and his mother. God acted by trusting in Joseph's creative courage. Arriving in Bethlehem and finding no lodging where Mary could give birth, Joseph took a stable and, as best he could, turned it into a welcoming home for the Son of God come into the world (cf. Lk 2:6–7). Faced with imminent danger from Herod, who wanted to kill the child, Joseph was warned once again in a dream to protect the child, and rose in the middle of the night to prepare the flight into Egypt (cf. Mt 2:13–14). A superficial reading of these stories can often give the impression that the world is at the mercy of the strong and mighty, but the "good news" of the Gospel consists in showing that, for all the arrogance and violence of worldly powers, God always finds a way to carry out his saving plan. So too, our lives may at times seem to be at the mercy of the powerful, but the Gospel shows us what counts. God always finds a way to save us, provided we show the same creative courage as the carpenter of Nazareth, who was able to turn a problem into a possibility by trusting always in divine providence.

THE GOSPEL DOES not tell us how long Mary, Joseph and the child remained in Egypt. Yet they certainly needed to eat, to find a home and employment. It does not take much imagination to fill in those details. The Holy Family had to face concrete problems like every other family, like so many of our migrant brothers and sisters who, today too, risk their lives to escape misfortune and hunger. In this regard, I consider Saint Joseph the special patron of all those forced to leave their native lands because of war, hatred, persecution and poverty.

At the end of every account in which Joseph plays a role, the Gospel tells us that he gets up, takes the child and his mother, and does what God commanded him (cf. Mt 1:24; 2:14.21). Indeed, Jesus and Mary his Mother are the most precious treasure of our faith.

WE SHOULD ALWAYS consider whether we ourselves are protecting Jesus and Mary, for they are also mysteriously entrusted to our own responsibility, care and safekeeping. The Son of the Almighty came into our world in a state of great vulnerability. He needed to be defended, protected, cared for and raised by Joseph. God trusted Joseph, as did Mary, who found in him someone who would not only save her life but would always provide for her and her child.

In this sense, Saint Joseph could not be other than the Guardian of the Church, for the Church is the continuation of the Body of Christ in history, even as Mary's motherhood is reflected in the motherhood of the Church. In his continued protection of the Church, Joseph continues to protect the child and his mother, and we too, by our love for the Church, continue to love the child and his mother.

THAT CHILD WOULD go on to say: "As you did it to one of the least of these who are members of my family, you did it to me" (Mt 25:40). Consequently, every poor, needy, suffering or dying person, every stranger, every prisoner, every infirm person is "the child" whom Joseph continues to protect. For this reason, Saint Joseph is invoked as protector of the unfortunate, the needy, exiles, the afflicted, the poor and the dying. Consequently, the Church cannot fail to show a special love for the least of our brothers and sisters, for Jesus showed a particular concern for them and personally identified with them. From Saint Joseph, we must learn that same care and responsibility. We must learn to love the child and his mother, to love the sacraments and charity, to love the Church and the poor. Each of these realities is always the child and his mother.

SAINT JOSEPH WAS a carpenter who earned an honest living to provide for his family. From him, Jesus learned the value, the dignity and the joy of what it means to eat bread that is the fruit of one's own labor.

In our own day, when employment has once more become a burning social issue, and unemployment at times reaches record levels even in nations that for decades have enjoyed a certain degree of prosperity, there is a renewed need to appreciate the importance of dignified work, of which Saint Joseph is an exemplary patron.

Work is a means of participating in the work of salvation, an opportunity to hasten the coming of the Kingdom, to develop our talents and abilities, and to put them at the service of society and fraternal communion. It becomes an opportunity for the fulfilment not only of oneself, but also of that primary cell of society which is the family. A family without work is particularly vulnerable to difficulties, tensions, estrangement and even break-up. How can we speak of human dignity without working to ensure that everyone is able to earn a decent living?

WORKING PERSONS, whatever their job may be, are cooperating with God himself, and in some way become creators of the world around us. The crisis of our time, which is economic, social, cultural and spiritual, can serve as a summons for all of us to rediscover the value, the importance and necessity of work for bringing about a new "normal" from which no one is excluded. Saint Joseph's work reminds us that God himself, in becoming man, did not disdain work. The loss of employment that affects so many of our brothers and sisters and has increased as a result of the COVID-19 pandemic, should serve as a summons to review our priorities. Let us implore Saint Joseph the Worker to help us find ways to express our firm conviction that no young person, no person at all, no family should be without work!

FATHERS ARE NOT born but made. A man does not become a father simply by bringing a child into the world, but by taking up the responsibility to care for that child. Whenever a man accepts responsibility for the life of another, in some way he becomes a father to that person.

BEING A FATHER entails introducing children to life and reality. Not holding them back, being overprotective or possessive, but rather making them capable of deciding for themselves, enjoying freedom and exploring new possibilities. Perhaps for this reason, Joseph is traditionally called a "most chaste" father. That title is not simply a sign of affection, but the summation of an attitude that is the opposite of possessiveness.

Chastity is freedom from possessiveness in every sphere of one's life. Only when love is chaste, is it truly love. A possessive love ultimately becomes dangerous: it imprisons, constricts and makes for misery. God himself loved humanity with a chaste love; he left us free even to go astray and set ourselves against him. The logic of love is always the logic of freedom, and Joseph knew how to love with extraordinary freedom. He never made himself the center of things. He did not think of himself but focused instead on the lives of Mary and Jesus.

JOSEPH FOUND happiness not in mere self-sacrifice but in self-gift. In him, we never see frustration but only trust. His patient silence was the prelude to concrete expressions of trust. Our world today needs fathers. It has no use for tyrants who would domineer others as a means of compensating for their own needs. It rejects those who confuse authority with authoritarianism, service with servility, discussion with oppression, charity with a welfare mentality, power with destruction.

Every true vocation is born of the gift of oneself, which is the fruit of mature sacrifice. The priesthood and consecrated life likewise require this kind of maturity. Whatever our vocation, whether to marriage, celibacy or virginity, our gift of self will not come to fulfilment if it stops at sacrifice; were that the case, instead of becoming a sign of the beauty and joy of love, the gift of self would risk being an expression of unhappiness, sadness and frustration.

WHEN FATHERS refuse to live the lives of their children for them, new and unexpected vistas open up. Every child is the bearer of a unique mystery that can only be brought to light with the help of a father who respects that child's freedom. A father who realizes that he is most a father and educator at the point when he becomes "useless," when he sees that his child has become independent and can walk the paths of life unaccompanied. When he becomes like Joseph, who always knew that his child was not his own but had merely been entrusted to his care. In the end, this is what Jesus would have us understand when he says: "Call no man your father on earth, for you have one Father, who is in heaven" (Mt 23:9).

In every exercise of our fatherhood, we should always keep in mind that it has nothing to do with possession but is rather a "sign" pointing to a greater fatherhood. In a way, we are all like Joseph: a shadow of the heavenly Father, who "makes his sun rise on the evil and on the good, and sends rain on the just and on the unjust" (Mt 5:45). And a shadow that follows his Son.

Prayers to St. Joseph

PRAYER FOR
OUR CONVERSION

Hail, Guardian of the Redeemer,
Spouse of the Blessed Virgin Mary.
To you God entrusted his only Son;
in you Mary placed her trust;
with you Christ became man.

Blessed Joseph, to us too,
show yourself a father
and guide us in the path of life.
Obtain for us grace, mercy and courage,
and defend us from every evil. Amen.

—*Pope Francis*

MORNING PRAYER
TO ST. JOSEPH[2]

"Glorious Patriarch Saint Joseph, whose power
makes the impossible possible, come to my aid
in these times of anguish and difficulty. Take
under your protection the serious and troubling
situations that I commend to you, that they
may have a happy outcome. My beloved father,
all my trust is in you. Let it not be said that I
invoked you in vain, and since you can do everything with Jesus and Mary, show me that your
goodness is as great as your power. Amen."

---

2.   Every day, for over forty years, following Lauds I have recited
a prayer to Saint Joseph taken from a nineteenth-century French
prayer book of the Congregation of the Sisters of Jesus and Mary. It
expresses devotion and trust, and even poses a certain challenge to
Saint Joseph.

LITANY TO SAINT JOSEPH

Lord, have mercy	Lord, have mercy.
Christ, have mercy.	Christ, have mercy.
God the Son, Redeemer of the world,	have mercy on us.
God the Holy Spirit,	have mercy on us.
Holy Trinity, one God,	have mercy on us.
Holy Mary,	pray for us.
Saint Joseph,	pray for us.
Noble son of the House of David,	pray for us.
Light of patriarchs,	pray for us.
Husband of the Mother of God,	pray for us.
Guardian of the Virgin,	pray for us.

Foster father of the Son of God,

> pray for us.

Faithful guardian of Christ,   pray for us.

Head of the Holy Family,   pray for us.

Joseph, chaste and just,   pray for us.

Joseph, prudent and brave,   pray for us.

Joseph, obedient and loyal,   pray for us.

Pattern of patience,   pray for us.

Lover of poverty,   pray for us.

Model of workers,   pray for us.

Example to parents,   pray for us.

Guardian of virgins,   pray for us.

Pillar of family life,   pray for us.

Comfort of the troubled,   pray for us.

Hope of the sick,   pray for us.

Patron of the dying,   pray for us.

Terror of evil spirits,   pray for us.

Protector of the Church,   pray for us.

Lamb of God, you take away the sins of the
world,   have mercy on us.

Lamb of God, you take away the sins of the
world,   have mercy on us.

Let us pray.

O God, who in your inexpressible providence
were pleased to choose Saint Joseph
as spouse of the most holy Mother of your Son,
grant, we pray,
that we, who revere him as our protector on
earth,
may be worthy of his heavenly intercession.
Through Christ our Lord.

(During the Year of Saint Joseph, this litany is
ordinarily enriched with a partial indulgence
[Manual of Indulgences, conc. 22]. During the
Year of Saint Joseph, however—which lasts

from December 8, 2020 to December 8, 2021—
the use of the Litany of Saint Joseph has been
included among other prayers to St. Joseph
enriched with a plenary indulgence
[see Decree of the Apostolic Penitentiary issued
Dec. 8, 2020, section E], which may be earned
once a day subject to the usual conditions:
sacramental confession, reception of Holy
Communion, prayer for the intentions of
the Pope, and a total detachment to all sin,
including venial sin.)

PRAYER TO ST. JOSEPH FOR WORKERS AND THOSE SEEKING EMPLOYMENT

Silent and well-known carpenter in Nazareth,

model of workers, by the work of your hands

you gave your contribution to the work of the Creator,

you earned your living, and you provided for the needs of the Holy Family.

Intercede for all workers, in the difficulties of their daily lives,

especially for the unemployed, in their anxieties for tomorrow,

so that through the guidance of God, the great Architect and Builder,

they all may use their strength and talents to make visible God's new creation,

to offer a concrete service to society,

and to earn wages worthy of their efforts.

PRAYER TO SAINT JOSEPH
BY POPE JOHN PAUL II

Saint Joseph, with you, we bless the Lord.

God chose you from among all men of that time

to be the chaste spouse of Mary.

You stood at the threshold of the mystery of her divine maternity,

and with her, accepted it in faith

as the working of the Holy Spirit.

Because you became his father according to the Mosaic law,

Jesus was rooted in the line of David.

You constantly watched over the Mother and Child

with an affectionate care which protected their lives

and freed them to fulfill their destiny.

The Savior Jesus submitted himself to your fatherly guidance

throughout his childhood and adolescence.

You taught him the ins and outs of human existence,

and you remained part of his life, respecting its mysterious ways.

You are still at his side.

Continue to protect the whole Church,

the family which came into existence through the salvation wrought by Jesus.

[Protect especially the people of Canada, who have placed themselves under your patronage.]

Help the Church to come closer to the mystery of Christ

in that attitude of faith, and acceptance, and love that was your own.

Receive the spiritual and material requests of
all those who beg your intercession,

particularly families and those who are needy—
in every sense of that word.

Through you, they are certain to experience the
maternal gaze of Mary

and the hand of Jesus to assist them. Amen.

*(FROM ST. JOSEPH ORATORY OF MOUNT ROYAL,
MONTREAL, CANADA)*

PRAYER TO JOSEPH
FOR A HAPPY DEATH

St. Joseph, protector of the dying,

I ask you to intercede for all the dying

And I invoke your assistance in the hour of my own death.

You merited a happy passing by a holy life

And in your last hours

You had the great consolation of being assisted by Jesus and Mary.

Deliver me from sudden death;

Obtain for me the grace to imitate you in life

To detach my heart from everything worldly

And daily to gather treasures for the moment of my death.

Obtain for me the grace to receive the sacrament of the sick well,

And with Mary, fill my heart

with sentiments of faith, hope, love and sorrow for my sins

so that I may breathe forth my soul in peace. Amen.

FEAST OF ST. JOSEPH, SPOUSE OF THE BLESSED VIRGIN MARY, MARCH 19

Grant,

We Pray, almighty God,

That by St. Joseph's intercession

Your Church may constantly watch over

The unfolding of the mysteries of human salvation,

whose beginning you entrusted to his faithful care.

FEAST OF ST. JOSEPH
THE WORKER, MAY 1

O God, Creator of all things,

Who laid down for the human race the law of work,

Graciously grant

That by the example of St. Joseph and under his patronage

We may complete the works you set us to do

And attain the rewards you promise.

PRAYER TO ST. JOSEPH
BY ST. JOHN HENRY NEWMAN

FIRST DAY

Consider the Glorious Titles of St. Joseph
He was the true and worthy Spouse of Mary,
supplying in a visible manner the place of
Mary's Invisible Spouse, the Holy Ghost. He was
a virgin, and his virginity was the faithful mirror
of the virginity of Mary. He was the Cherub,
placed to guard the new terrestrial Paradise
from the intrusion of every foe.

V. Blessed be the name of Joseph.
R. Henceforth and forever. Amen.

Let us pray.

God, who in Thine ineffable Providence didst
vouchsafe to choose Blessed Joseph to be the
husband of Thy most holy Mother, grant, we
beseech Thee, that we may be made worthy to
receive him for our intercessor in heaven, whom
on earth we venerate as our holy Protector: who
livest and reignest world without end. Amen.

SECOND DAY

Consider the Glorious Titles of St. Joseph
His was the title of father of the Son of God, because he was the Spouse of Mary, ever Virgin. He was our Lord's father, because Jesus ever yielded to him the obedience of a son. He was our Lord's father, because to him were entrusted, and by him were faithfully fulfilled, the duties of a father, in protecting Him, giving Him a home, sustaining and rearing Him, and providing Him with a trade.

V. Blessed be the name of Joseph.
R. Henceforth and forever. Amen.

Let us pray.

God, who in Thine ineffable Providence didst vouchsafe to choose Blessed Joseph to be the husband of Thy most holy Mother, grant, we beseech Thee, that we may be made worthy to receive him for our intercessor in heaven, whom on earth we venerate as our holy Protector: who livest and reignest world without end. Amen.

THIRD DAY

Consider the Glorious Titles of St. Joseph
He is Holy Joseph, because according to the
opinion of a great number of doctors, he, as
well as St. John the Baptist, was sanctified even
before he was born. He is Holy Joseph, because
his office, of being spouse and protector of Mary,
specially demanded sanctity. He is Holy Joseph,
because no other Saint but he lived in such and
so long intimacy and familiarity with the source
of all holiness, Jesus, God incarnate, and Mary,
the holiest of creatures.

V. Blessed be the name of Joseph.
R. Henceforth and forever. Amen.

Let us pray.

God, who in Thine ineffable Providence didst
vouchsafe to choose Blessed Joseph to be the
husband of Thy most holy Mother, grant, we
beseech Thee, that we may be made worthy to
receive him for our intercessor in heaven, whom
on earth we venerate as our holy Protector: who
livest and reignest world without end. Amen.

BYZANTINE CATHOLIC HYMN
TO ST. JOSEPH

O holy and righteous Joseph! While yet on earth, you did have boldness before the Son of God, Who was well pleased to call you His father, in that you were the betrothed of His Mother, and Who was well pleased to be obedient to you. We believe that as you do dwell now in the heavenly mansions with the choirs of the righteous, you are listened to, in all that you do request from our God and Savior.

Therefore, fleeing to your protection and defense, we beg and humbly entreat you: as you, yourself, were delivered from a storm of doubting thoughts, so also deliver us that are tempest-tossed by the waves of confusion and passions; as you did shield the all-Pure Virgin from the slanders of men, so shield us from all kinds of vehement calumny; as you did keep the incarnate Lord from all harm and affliction, so also by your defense preserve His Church and all of us from all affliction and harm.

You know, O Saint of God, that even the Son of God had bodily needs in the days of His incarnation, and you did attend to them. Therefore, we beseech you: tend, yourself, to our temporal needs through your intercession, granting us every good thing, which is needful in this life (for the sake of life of the age to come).

Especially, do we entreat you to intercede that we may receive remission of our sins from Him Who was called your Son, the only-begotten Son of God, our Lord Jesus Christ, and be worthy of inheriting the Kingdom of Heaven, so that, abiding with you in the heavenly mansions, we may ever glorify the One God in three Persons: the † Father, the Son and the Holy Spirit, now and for ever, and unto the ages of ages.

ST. TERESA OF AVILA
ON DEVOTION TO ST. JOSEPH

"I took for my advocate and lord the glorious Saint Joseph and commended myself earnestly to him; and I found that this my father and lord delivered me both from this trouble and also from other and greater troubles concerning my honor and the loss of my soul, and that he gave me greater blessings than I could ask of him. I do not remember even now that I have ever asked anything of him which he has failed to grant. I am astonished at the great favors which God has bestowed on me through this blessed saint, and at the perils from which He has freed me, both in body and in soul. To other saints the Lord seems to have given grace to succor us in some of our necessities but of this glorious saint my experience is that he succors us in them all and that the Lord wishes to teach us that as He was Himself subject to him on earth (for, being His guardian and being called His father, he could command Him) just so in Heaven He still does all that he asks. This has also been the experience of other persons whom I have advised to commend themselves to him; and even to-day there are many who have great devotion to him through having newly experienced this truth."

"I wish I could persuade everyone to be devoted to this glorious saint, for I have great experience of the blessings which he can obtain from God. I have never known anyone to be truly devoted to him and render him particular services who did not notably advance in virtue, for he gives very real help to souls who commend themselves to him. For some years now, I think, I have made some request of him every year on his festival and I have always had it granted. If my petition is in any way ill directed, he directs it aright for my greater good."

"I only beg, for the love of God, that anyone who does not believe me will put what I say to the test, and he will see by experience what great advantages come from his commending himself to this glorious patriarch and having devotion to him. Those who practice prayer should have a special affection for him always. I do not know how anyone can think of the Queen of the Angels, during the time that she suffered so much with the Child Jesus, without giving thanks to Saint Joseph for the way he helped them. If anyone cannot find a master to teach him how to pray, let him take this glorious saint as his master and he will not go astray." (Autobiography, Chapter 6)

ART CREDITS